❦ BOOK REVIEW

The book is sure to appeal to both the numerous fans of Encyclopedia Brown and those who enjoy the equally popular trivia books.

from SCHOOL LIBRARY JOURNAL

Weekly Reader Books presents

Encyclopedia Brown's Book of Wacky CARS

DONALD J. SOBOL

Illustrated by Ted Enik

WILLIAM MORROW AND COMPANY, INC.
New York

AUTHOR'S NOTE
All the stories in this book are true.
—DONALD J. SOBOL

This book is a presentation of Weekly Reader Books.
Weekly Reader Books offers book clubs for children
from preschool through high school. For further
information write to: **Weekly Reader Books,**
4343 Equity Drive, Columbus, Ohio 43228.

Published by arrangement with William Morrow and Company, Inc.
Weekly Reader is a trademark of Field Publications.
Printed in the United States of America.

Library of Congress Cataloging-in-Publication Data

Sobol, Donald J., 1924– Encyclopedia Brown's book of wacky cars.

Summary: True, wacky stories about cars—famous cars, unusual cars, vintage cars,
impractical cars, and others.
1. Automobiles—Juvenile humor. [1. Automobiles—Anecdotes] I. Enik, Ted, ill.
II. Title. TL147.S63 1987   629.2'222'0207   86–23556
ISBN 0–688–06222–9

For
Mildred Platt,
and to the memory
of
Sydney Platt

Contents

Encyclopedia Brown's
Book of Wacky
CARS

Introduction

Every year in July, the town of Idaville auctions off unclaimed and unwanted property. Bikes, televisions, office furniture, boats, and even cars are put up for sale.

On the day of the auction, Encyclopedia and his junior partner, Sally Kimball, closed the Brown Detective Agency early. They biked to the police garage on Third Street to say hello to good buys. A crowd of grown-ups and children was already there.

Sally nodded at two used police cars parked along the rear wall.

"Who would buy an old police car?" she wondered.

"Taxicab companies in large cities," Encyclopedia replied. "A small-town police car in good condition is a prize find."

"Why?" Sally said.

"Police cars are tough. They're equipped with everything heavy-duty, including frame, brakes, tires, and shock absorbers," Encyclopedia explained. "Naturally, before they become taxicabs, a few changes have to be made, such as—"

"Hey, did you see the fishing trophy?" a voice interrupted.

It was Monroe Burnside. Monroe collected trophies. He didn't win them, he just collected them.

Encyclopedia looked where Monroe pointed. On a rolltop desk nearby was a white ashtray with a tiny figure of a fisherman on the rim. The words *Bonefishing Tournament First Place 1968* were printed on the base.

"If it goes for less than a dollar, I have a chance to own it," Monroe said. "Isn't it beautiful!"

"It's lovely," Sally agreed in a strained tone. "Don't worry. You'll get it."

"I'm not so sure," Monroe said gravely. "Conway Tintushel is here. He's crazy about fishing. He'd bid on a wet line."

Monroe was right. Conway thought about fishing more than anything else. Whenever he turned on a drinking fountain at school, he cried, "Thar she blows!"

Encyclopedia and Sally wished Monroe good luck and walked toward the used police cars.

Sally said, "Oh, boy, is that figure of a fisherman ever ugly. It's enough to make a person give up fishing. Who'd want the ashtray besides Monroe and Conway?"

"Someone who wants to give up smoking," Encyclopedia suggested.

Several men were examining the police cars. They looked under the hood, peered at the upholstery, and checked the mileage.

The detectives joined them. Soon afterward, the auctioneer called, "All right, folks, we're ready to start."

The crowd moved to the front of the garage. The auctioneer, a tall, thin man, stood behind a high table. For a couple of minutes, he talked about the fine condition of all the items on sale. Then he opened the bidding.

He had sold nine chairs, five file cabinets, and a rubber lifeboat when Monroe Burnside appeared beside Encyclopedia.

"Come quickly," Monroe urged.

Encyclopedia motioned to Sally. The detectives followed Monroe behind the two police cars at the back of the garage.

Conway Tintushel was there. He was holding the ashtray with the figure of a fisherman.

"I caught him trying to steal it," Monroe said.

"Don't listen to him, Encyclopedia," Conway blurted. "He's running on empty. *I* caught *him* trying to get out the window with it."

"Liar!" exclaimed Monroe. "If people needed a license to tell the truth, you'd have to ask for a learner's permit!"

"Hold on, both of you," Encyclopedia said. "You'll each have a chance to tell your story. You first, Monroe."

"A couple of minutes ago I started for the rest room,"

Monroe said. "As I passed on the far side of the two police cars, I heard a noise. Conway was sneaking out the back door of the first car with the ashtray in his hand. So I followed him. He went to the rear exit of the garage and tried to get away. I stopped him and ran to get you, Encyclopedia."

Encyclopedia turned to Conway. "What do you have to say?"

"I was never in the police car," Conway said. "I was walking back toward the rest room when I saw Monroe crouched between one of the cars and the back wall. He was carrying the ashtray. But when he saw me, he shoved it into my hands and asked me to hold it a minute. Then he ran and got you."

"Let's walk a bit," Encyclopedia said to Sally.

The detectives moved off until they were out of earshot of Monroe and Conway.

"Who do you think tried to steal the ashtray?" Encyclopedia asked.

"I don't know," Sally said. "Monroe could be trying to frame Conway. Conway could be trying to frame Monroe. Either could have swiped the ashtray when no one was looking."

"And hidden in or behind the police car," Encyclopedia said. "When the auction began, everyone was facing the other way. That's when the thief tried to run for the rear exit."

"But that doesn't tell us which one is the thief," Sally said, "Monroe or Conway?"

5

"If we only had a clue," Encyclopedia murmured thoughtfully.

"What was Conway doing in the police car?" Sally said. "It doesn't make sense, unless he hid in the car till he thought the coast was clear. He might have escaped with the ashtray except that Monroe saw him."

Sally shook her head, puzzled.

"Of course, Monroe could be lying and Conway could be telling the truth," she went on. "Monroe could be the thief or Conway could be the thief. Good heavens, I can't spot a single clue."

Encyclopedia's face lit up. "That's it! That's the answer. The clue is what's *missing!*"

"Encyclopedia, stop it. Who's guilty, Monroe or Conway?"

Encyclopedia told her.

Sally gasped. She stared at the two police cars. "Why didn't I see that! Golly, Encyclopedia, you ought to start a collection of odd things about cars. Funny things."

"I already have," Encyclopedia said.

After the auction, the detectives returned to Encyclopedia's garage, home of the Brown Detective Agency.

On the back wall were shelves with several scrapbooks. Sally had already seen a few of them—the collections of wacky crimes, wacky spies, wacky sports, and wacky animals.

Encyclopedia passed over these and took down a brown scrapbook. He laid it on the desk.

6

"My collection of true, wacky stories about cars," he said proudly.

Sally opened the scrapbook eagerly and began to read. . . .

(To find out which boy tried to steal the ashtray with the figure of the fisherman, turn to page 115.)

I

Wacky Cars

Down in front! Advertisements termed the Duck "the newest, latest, best thing ever produced in the auto line."

What it produced was a clunk. It laid the biggest egg of any car ever offered to the American public.

Believe it or not, the driver sat in the rear, where the pedals and steering wheel were located. Passengers sat on folding seats in front of him and blocked his view of the road.

The Duck was built in 1913 by the Jackson Motor Company of Jackson, Michigan. Practical features weren't a Jackson speciality. Its 1910 Rambler Surrey had headlights that doubled as bumpers!

That's one big pizza car. The biggest car ever manufactured for personal use was the Bugatti Royale. It weighed 7,000 pounds, more than twice the weight of the average American car. And it was as long as your living room—if your living room is 20 to 22 feet long.

The Royale was built in France by an Italian, Ettore Arco Isidoro Bugatti, between 1927 and 1933. The chassis sold for around $25,000. Each body was different, being built to the customer's wishes, and cost up to $20,000 extra.

The cars were works of art. With the passing years, they became more and more valuable. Oh, my, did they ever!

On June 27, 1986, a 1931 Bugatti Royale Berline de Voyage was sold in Reno, Nevada, for $6.5 million, the highest price ever paid at auction for an automobile.

"I was happy to buy it for less than ten million," said the winning bidder, Jerry J. Moore, 58, a Houston shopping-center developer. Before the auction, he had called the Bugatti a "very ugly car, but ugly enough to be unusual."

His yellow-and-black hunk of iron and wood, with its convertible-roofed chauffeur's compartment, is long on luxury and short on economy. The 300-horsepower, 778-cubic inch straight-eight engine slurps a gallon of gas every 6 miles and sounds like an old diesel truck. The car cost $42,000 new and once was resold for $1,500!

Probably no more than eight Bugatti Royales were made. Besides Moore's, five others still exist. But if you long to be the first on your street to own one, you're in

for a disappointment. The others are locked in museums and private collections.

"I don't think there will be another one available for the next two hundred years," said Moore.

And it only ran on Union Oil. The city of Hartford, Michigan, had a police car that shared a trait with many humans. It didn't like to work on Saturdays and Sundays.

The car was a 1982 Plymouth, and before it was more than a few months old, it had already been to the repair shop eight times to be treated for weekend blahs.

"You can be driving down the road and the engine stops running without any warning," said a city official. "The oddest thing is that it only happens on weekends. I guess it doesn't like to work overtime."

He wasn't dune too well. Once upon a time a man known simply as Dr. Bischoff lived in Kiel, Germany. Daily he gazed upon the waters of the Baltic.

Out of such gazing came the inspiration to invent a ship—not an ocean liner, of which there were plenty, but a *desert* liner.

By 1927, plans for the "Ship of the Desert" were completed. It would be four stories high, 60 yards long, and weigh 350 tons. Driven by a 200-horsepower ship's engine, it would plow the billowy wastes of the Sahara on wheels 15 yards in diameter.

To get the monstrous dune buggy off the drawing

11

board and onto the sand, Bischoff formed a company and set about raising money.

Three models were offered: a passenger ship, a freighter, and a ship-of-war. In varying degrees of luxury, all three models would have such comforts as baths, ventilators, and dining and sleeping quarters.

Bischoff's sales pitch rocked the imagination but raised no money. With doubt as its sole cargo, the Ship of the Desert sank quietly into the sands of time.

Giant car sail. In 1910, the wind-powered automobile had a moment in the sun.

The machine was a light frame supporting a saddle and a mast. The whole rested upon four wheels: a large wheel front and back, and a smaller wheel on either side. The wheels in the rear and on the right side were rigidly connected, as were the ones in front and on the left. The driver-sailor steered by pressing his feet on the width-wise axle. His hands remained free to work the sail or to brake.

The windmobile was expected to go over big with lovers of sport. "Contests of speed," reported one newspaper with empty columns to fill, "will involve but little of the dangers of cycle or automobile races." What counted most were the quickness and skill "required in using to the utmost the surrounding air conditions."

A patent on the windmobile was taken out by a person who ranks among history's wrong-way thinkers.

13

American newspapers described him merely as "a German inventor."

"He is," wrote a New York reporter, "a man who desired to become an airplane pilot but feared to fall."

The car that never was. Craig Hinton, a car specialist for moviemakers, insists that he once owned the two best Mercedes ever built. They were Jaguars.

The producers of the film *Raiders of the Lost Ark* needed a 1936 German staff car, a Mercedes. They called Hinton.

Hinton couldn't find the real thing. So in May 1980, he and his crew went to work in a garage near Coventry, England. In twelve weeks they built a 1936 Mercedes body on a 1960 Jaguar chassis. A backup model took two weeks longer.

Outwardly, the "Jag-cedes" were identical to the originals down to the pleats in the upholstery. Inwardly, they were better. The 1936 Mercedes had a top speed of 70 m.p.h. Powered by the newer Jaguar engines, the two look-alikes zipped along at 120 m.p.h.

The filmmakers took the first car to Tunisia for a scene in which a mad Nazi and his men engage in a spectacular desert chase. Hinton brought the second car over three weeks later.

From the moment he drove the "Jag-cede" off the dock, he got attention. Wherever he went, he was greeted with the respect normally paid a chief of state. Men and women smiled and waved at the 1936 German staff car with its jet-black paint and split windshield.

15

Police came to attention as it sped by. Soldiers saluted.

Hinton was flattered but puzzled. He knew the car was good. But how could people on the side of the road appreciate his craftsmanship at a glance?

Eventually he learned the reason for all the acclaim.

There was another 1936 German staff car in Tunisia —an original one—and it belonged to the president of the country.

Advance to the rear. A German scout car was captured by the Americans in Southern Tunisia during World War II. It had eight wheels, two drivers, and never had to turn around.

16

It also had two front ends.

One driver sat in the front and the other . . . er, in the front. The car could speed forward in any direction at speeds faster than 50 m.p.h.

The Americans painted a white star over the German cross and used the car for reconnaissance purposes. It proved battle-worthy, though no one inside it ever knew for certain if he was advancing or retreating.

Beetle blooper. After World War II, the Volkswagen factory in Germany was inspected by American and British experts. They were asked if it was worth taking over as payment, in part, for war damages.

Volkswagen's sole product was the Beetle, an automobile that was designed in 1938 as a "people's car" for German workers.

The ugly little car was scoffed at.

"This car is not worth a darn," said the head of the American group, Ernest Breech, president of the Ford Motor Company. The British experts held the same view.

So the Germans kept the factory and produced the Beetle in many countries. By 1972, the little auto had become the best-selling single-model car ever, with more than 15 million sold around the world.

Let the driver beware. Juan Perón, once the dictator of Argentina, ran his country and his cars with equal cunning.

As a gift to his wife, Eva, he ordered a 1952 Rolls-Royce. It was bulletproof, but only for the passengers. The driver's compartment was unarmored.

Perón figured that a driver would refuse to take a bribe to steer the car into an ambush if he knew he was unprotected.

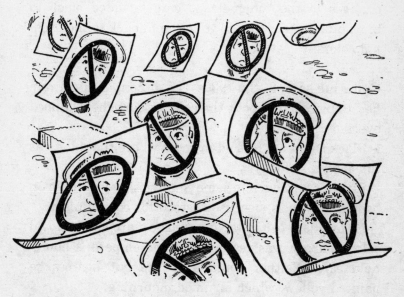

Inside job. Leaflets opposing Benito Mussolini, the Fascist premier of Italy from 1922 to 1943, appeared mysteriously in the streets of Italy's largest cities in 1930.

The leaflets seemed to come from nowhere. Suddenly they were flying around in the midst of heavy traffic.

Several cars had been fitted with propellers on the exhaust. The wind blew out the anti-Mussolini leaflets from a hidden chamber like bullets from a gun.

19

Follow that black, uh . . . blue, uh . . . never mind.
Hits of the 1929 Automobile Salon at the Commodore
Hotel in New York City were cars finished in colors
that changed under different lighting.

The cars on exhibition all had custom-built bodies by
American and European coachwork makers. Color
changes in the "chameleon" cars included black to
blue, blue to gray, tan to yellow, and back to the original colors.

Color me safe. In the 1930s, U.S. auto manufacturers
had to be careful about the color of cars they shipped
overseas.

Black could not be sold in India where the color was
considered unlucky.

Red was forbidden in some countries, even as trim on
body and wheels, because it stood for communism.

No ordinary car in Japan could be maroon. The royal
color, maroon was reserved for the emperor's house-
hold cars. Neither could any cars but hearses be
painted yellow, which signified mourning.

Overkill. The Law Enforcement Assistance Adminis-
tration decided to make the policeman's job easier in
the mid-1970s by bringing the patrol car up to date.

A Chevrolet was borrowed from the New Orleans
Police Department and outfitted with nearly $2 million
worth of electronic equipment.

Included in the souping up was a TV monitor, a mul-
tiple-spark discharge system, tire sensors, a voice/digi-

tal terminal, and a microcomputer electronic system.

The shortcoming was human. There was too much to watch *inside* the car. Besides, the policeman had to hook himself into the system. That made quick exits as easy as wiggling out of a straitjacket.

Plans to equip ten patrol cars and test them in police departments across the country were scrapped. The one-of-a-kind supercar was stripped down and returned to New Orleans.

There it resumed life as an ordinary Chevy patrol car.

Life in the slow lane. An English businessman gave up his Rolls-Royce to drive a mechanical shovel.

Robin Goforth of Doncaster bought the yellow five-ton construction vehicle for about $42,000 at an auction in 1985. He tried unsuccessfully to unload his 1972 Rolls Corniche convertible, worth about $35,000, at the same auction. It didn't bring a high enough bid.

Goforth said he was afraid to drive the Rolls into town. It was too much of a temptation for thieves and vandals.

"The shovel will stand up to anything short of an earthquake," he said. "And it's easier to steer than the Rolls."

Absolutely no rust. The most valuable car ever built is yours for free.

If you can overlook a top speed of a little over eight miles an hour, see what you're getting.

A superb, custom-built, fully loaded cream puff that is out of this world, a like-new roadster that cost $2 million to manufacture and has been driven less than 30 miles.

Standard goodies include six sets of hand tools worth $45,000 each, twelve motor-driven cameras worth around $40,000 each, and six complete TV cameras worth $90,000 each. Throw in all sorts of camping equipment and life-support systems.

Would you believe the first lunar rover? It was left behind when the American astronauts returned to earth from exploring and collecting rock samples.

All you have to do is pick it up where it's parked on the moon.

24

II

Loose Behind the Wheel

Look where we've been. James B. Hargis and Charles Creighton saw America backward.

They made a round trip from New York to California driving in reverse all the way—and without stopping their engine one time.

The two men left New York City on July 26, 1930. The trip took forty-two days. They arrived back in (or backed into) New York City, shut off the engine, and posed for pictures on September 7.

The gears of the car were reworked so it could move in reverse only, and headlights were attached to the rear. The only accident of the 7,180-mile journey occurred in the first mile. A taxicab dented a front fender and running board.

After a short stay in New York City, Hargis, an inte-

rior decorator, and Creighton, a mechanic, drove home to St. Louis in forward.

Double take. It began as an ordinary shopping trip.

Richard Baker took his wife in their 1978 American Motors maroon Concord to the Northgate Shopping Center in Sheboygan, Wisconsin, on April 1, 1985.

He came out before she did and put some groceries in the trunk. As he slid inside to drive from the parking space to pick her up, he discovered that his seat was mysteriously far back.

The couple was returning from another errand when Mrs. Baker said, "Something is wrong. Whose sunglasses are these? And look at all this stuff in here. This isn't our car!"

Baker got out and checked the license plate. They had the wrong car.

The couple drove back to the shopping center. The police were waiting for them. Six-foot four-inch Thomas J. Baker—no relation to Richard Baker—had reported the theft of his maroon 1978 Concord.

"The policeman was talking like I was going to try to get away with the car," Richard Baker said.

The officer changed his mind after trying the keys on the cars. Both keys unlocked and started both cars. Mystery solved.

"The odds are a minimum of ten thousand to one on just the keys fitting," declared Ben Dunn, an American Motors spokesman. "When you add the factors of the

27

color matching, the model and make being the same, the owners having the same last name, and both being in the same place on April Fool's Day, I can't even estimate the odds."

If life hands you a lemon, why, make lemonade. Or, as a fed-up owner did with his lemon of a car, beat it to a pulp.

Ricky Johnson of Gloucester, England, was snowed under by repair bills on his 1978 Rover. When the car died on his way to work in 1982, he thought, "Enough!"

He pushed the car off the road, took a sledgehammer from the trunk, and bashed in the rear window. He felt better and better as he smashed all the windows and started on the body. After twenty minutes of pounding, the Rover was a shapeless mass of metal.

"I'm real glad I did it," he said. "I got everything out of my system."

Two policemen in a patrol car stopped to investigate as Johnson was laying it on the Rover. They took no action.

"It was his property," said a police spokesman. "Besides, he had the car towed to a scrap yard when he was finished. He was quite responsible about the whole thing."

Aw, quit blubbering. Bella Petruccioli picked out a tiny sports car to test-drive—and got stuck so tight that firemen had to spend several hours cutting her loose.

Petruccioli, the 312-pound mother of three, waddled into a Fiat showroom outside of Rome, Italy, in 1985.

"I looked up and there was this huge lady eyeballing the teeniest car in the place," said Gino Romanazzi, a salesman. "I swear, she was bigger than the car."

Romanazzi tried to steer her to something more her size, but she wanted the little blue job. She waved a fistful of money. She said if he didn't let her take the car for a test drive, she'd buy a car somewhere else.

The salesman threw up his hands and told her to shove herself in there if she could. "I knew it was going to be a disaster," he said with a moan.

Petruccioli sucked in her belly, wiggled into the bucket seat, and exhaled. That's when she learned she was wedged fast.

"That fat lady was packed in there like ten pounds of lard in a five-pound can," said a customer, Tony Bulbarelli. He skipped a half day of work to stay and watch the spectacle. "Her front was draped over the steering wheel like a hen hunkered over an egg. You couldn't even see the wheel under all that blubber."

Petruccioli started screaming that she couldn't breathe and for someone to yank her out. Salesmen pushed and pulled and tried jiggling her free. She didn't budge.

The sales manager had an idea: Grease her and just slide her out. He was overruled. Firemen were called. They had to chop apart the poor little sports car to rescue her.

The Fiat dealer sued to recover the cost of the

wrecked car. The beefy Petruccioli said she wouldn't pay.

"They shouldn't make cars women can't get in and out of," she declared.

Taken to the cleaners. Lucia Ankram of London, England, drove a brand-new car in 1975—for about fifteen seconds.

Leaving the dealer's lot, she made a wrong turn down a one-way street and smashed through the display window of a dry-cleaning shop.

Those are the brakes. In Pomona, California, a 73-year-old woman passed her driver's test in 1985. As she started to drive home, her foot slipped from the brake pedal and onto the accelerator. The car shot whiz-bang across the parking lot and through the wall of the Department of Motor Vehicles.

By a miracle, no one was hurt. Only minutes earlier, a line of people waiting to take their driving test had stood along the wall struck by the car.

Less lucky was a woman in Harrisburg, Pennsylvania, in 1939. While completing the driver's test, she drove up three steps and crashed into the building where the licenses were issued.

State policeman J. P. Heck stamped a single word over her application: *Failed.*

And how!

Some like 'em shot. After singing idol Elvis Presley died, his favorite automobile was put up for sale in California in 1981.

Before it ever reached the auction block, a couple of gentlemen with a suitcase stuffed with jewels struck a private deal. They got the car for the gems—$2 million worth. The price was more than anyone had ever paid for street wheels.

The car, a 1971 Detomaso Pantera, featured a little something extra—a dashboard display of bullet holes. Presley, the king of rock and roll, shot up the machine one day when it wouldn't start.

On the wrong track. Richard Horan of Westwood, Massachusetts, parked his car on a quiet, snow-covered New Hampshire road in 1983. Sliding his snowmobile from the trailer, he scooted off for a day's fun.

He returned to an unpleasant surprise. His car and trailer looked exactly as if they'd been run over by a freight train.

They had been.

Unknowingly, Horan had parked on a part of the road that ran over the Maine Central Railroad tracks, which were hidden beneath the snow. The train couldn't be stopped in time to avoid a crunch.

When Horan came back to tow the wrecked car, he found insult added to injury.

On the windshield was a ticket for improper parking.

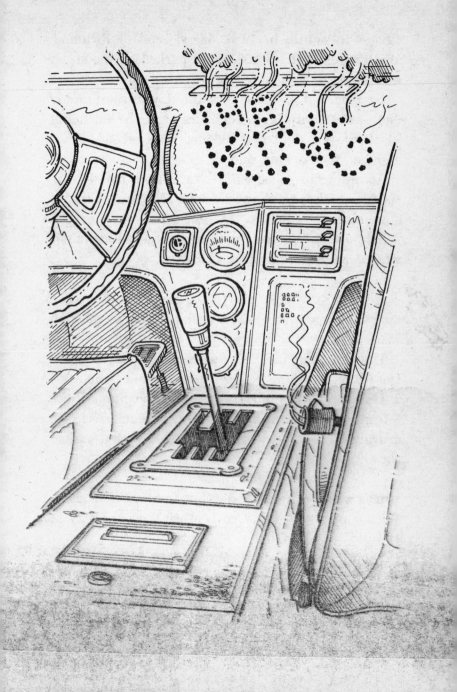

Learn to smile. In 1985, Jerry Todd of Richland, Washington, left his 1981 Ford parked on the street and joined a car pool to work.

He returned at the end of the day to see number eight—the eighth car in ten hours—ram the left side of his Ford. All eight cars skidded on a stretch of ice eighteen inches wide, and wham-o!

According to police officer Norm Conway, who responded to three of the accidents, "That's some kind of state record."

Said Todd, "You've got to have a sense of humor when your car is hit eight times."

Not ferry funny. A court in Denmark sentenced a man to five months in jail for drunk driving on the high seas.

The screwball incident occurred in 1982 aboard a Danish ferry sailing between Sweden and Denmark.

The man was feeling no pain when he climbed into a trailer truck parked on the ferry's vehicle deck. He drove back and forth until he collided with a parked car.

Guess who I ran into today? Two women of Wausau, Wisconsin, got to know each other the hard way in 1981.

Their cars collided at a Fifth Street intersection.

As the policemen packed up their paperwork on the fender-bender, the two women drove off in different directions.

Half a minute later they collided at an intersection a block away.

Watch out for doze curves. Sleep may be better than medicine for some. But for a 15-year-old boy in England, sleep was dangerous to his health. Police found the boy shivering in the middle of a road in Southampton on a cold December night in 1983. All he had on were his pajamas.

The boy explained his plight. He had gotten out of bed at his home in Portsmouth, walked to the car, and driven twenty-seven miles to Southampton—while fast asleep. He said he had never been behind the wheel of a car before.

His parents admitted that he had a history of sleepwalking.

Where's there's life . . . Dorothy Pearse of Ovendon, England, made Britain's front pages in 1983. She was pictured happily tearing up her learner's license tag.

More than 65 percent of first-timers flunk the British driver's test, one of the toughest in the world. Pearse showed how tough.

She passed, but it had taken fifteen attempts and twenty-three years.

That's a national record for stamina but not for determination. Another Englishwoman, Miriam Hargrave, whizzed through thirty-nine failures in eight

years before she passed the test in 1970 at the age of 77.

Noodles Ferrari. Old sports cars never die, they just stand and serve.

Mike Sheehan of Costa Mesa, California, couldn't bear the thought of parting with his sports car, a racy 1969 Ferrari convertible.

With the help of a professional artist, Sheehan cubed the car into a piece of furniture in 1982. A car crusher flattened it—minus its wheels and interior—into a 2' by 2' by 4', 1,000-pound chunk. The artist pounded the mess here and there, painted it a bright Ferrari red, mounted it on a base, and fixed a glass top on it.

Eureka, the perfect "carfee" table!

Sloman on the totem pole. For seventy years Lillian Sloman, 91, of Arundel, England, had driven without an accident or a ticket.

In 1984, a judge went out of his way to praise her spotless record. Then he canceled her license because she drove too slowly. Officially, Sloman was charged with causing traffic jams on highways by creeping along at a maddening 15 miles an hour.

III

The "Get-a-Horse!" Years

Hay, that's nice. The November 1905 issue of *Horseless Age* published stories by doctors relating their experiences with the automobile.

A doctor in Illinois wrote that he bought an auto in 1903 to replace his three horses. He reasoned that cars, like horses, required the loving touch.

So twice a week he raised the car on jacks to rest the tires and used a stove to warm the motor on chilly mornings.

Were there no fools, there would be no wise men. Jeers and cries of "Get a horse!" raked the ears of early motorists.

Before the twentieth century, the automobile was called a "rich man's toy" and other names too shocking

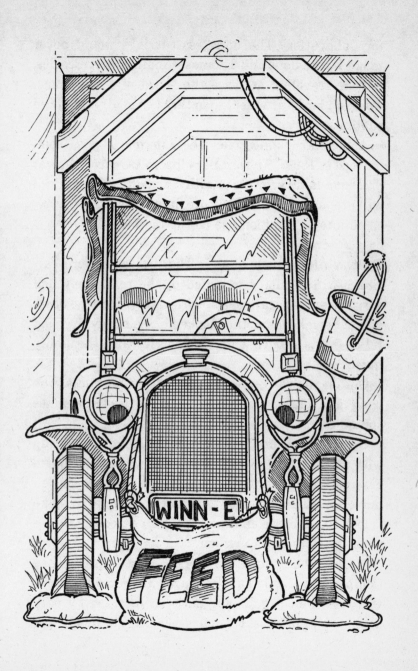

for publication. The horseless carriage would never make it, the doubting Thomases maintained. Besides, anyone traveling at twice the speed of a stagecoach wouldn't be able to breathe in the rush of air and would suffocate.

A popular publication, *The Literary Digest,* commented in 1889: "The ordinary 'horseless carriage' is at present a luxury for the wealthy; and although its price will probably fall in the future, it will never, of course, come into as common use as the bicycle."

Quit while you're ahead. The first cars were carriages with a motor mounted in the rear. They had carriage wheels, carriage springs, and a carriage dashboard. Seen head-on, they looked like a buggy that had rolled from the barn while Dad was fetching the family horse.

Out on the road, they were far from harmless. The bang and clatter and roar of two-cylinder engines spread terror among the horse population.

Uriah Smith of Battle Creek, Michigan, came up with an invention to make the roads safe for gas-burners and hay-burners alike. He fixed a life-size wooden horse's head and neck to the front of his auto to make it look like a horse and carriage. He named the rig his "Horsey Horseless Carriage."

In 1899, he formed the Horsey Horseless Carriage Company in Battle Creek. Alack, his horse-faced car was less than a galloping success. Rejected by both dobbins and drivers, it slipped headfirst into oblivion.

Name of the game. Automobiles were frequently named for the men who put America on wheels, such as Chevrolet, Chrysler, Dodge, and Ford. Next most common were the names of the cities and states in which the cars were made, such as Detroit, Chicago, and California.

Left over were enough names to satisfy just about every buyer.

Eight cars were named for presidents: Grant, Harding, Jackson, Johnson, Lincoln, Monroe, Roosevelt, and Washington.

Hunters had numerous cars with animal names to chose from, including Seven Little Buffaloes. Anglers had a Fish, a Brooks, and an Anchor.

Educators had a Harvard, a Columbia, and an Oxford. Blowhards had a Gale. Girl Scout leaders had a Brownie.

Surgeons cottoned to a Blood. Exterminators took "pest-drives" in a Bugmobile. Clock-watchers eyed the Elgin. Fatties drooled over a Calorie or an American Chocolate.

Practical jokers had an Imp or a Kidder. Communists had an Everybody's, and regional loyalists had a Southern, a Midwest, and a Dixie.

Buyers who needed help telling a car's front end from the rear went for a Frontmobile. Those who sought a hint on performance started shopping with a Quick, a Silent, a Speedwell, a U.S. Long Distance, or a Zip.

Those who longed to recapture their youth looked

first at a Lad's Car or a Peter Pan. For patriotic citizens, there were a Minute Man Six, an Independence, and a Liberty. Who, if his name was Hills, could resist a Beverly?

And for those who liked to troubleshoot, the choice was easiest of all: either a Klink or a Knox.

Great moments to remember. The first automobile show was held in New York City in 1900. The excited press called it a triumph "almost equal" to that of the yearly horse show.

And a lot cleaner.

Out on a toot. When the electric horn began to replace the old rubber squeeze bulb, the musical automobile was born.

Kaiser Wilhelm of Germany put five-tone horns on his cars in 1912. The melody could be heard four blocks away and warned citizens of Berlin that he was coming.

Only the Kaiser could blow his own horn; no one else in the land could have one like it. The company that made them pledged itself not to sell any more within Germany.

Just 4,000 more poles to San Francisco. Alice Huyler Ramsey was the first woman to drive an automobile across America. To guide herself, she read the telephone poles.

In 1909, Ramsey, 22, left New York City at the wheel of a Maxwell with three women passengers. Two months later, she arrived in San Francisco after a trip of 3,800 miles.

At that time, the country was still an automotive wilderness. Few good public roads existed. Road maps were five years in the future. Ramsey had to drive over Indian trails, along farm roads, and across plowed fields.

Fortunately, telephone poles—"crude and not very tall"—stretched from coast to coast. Ramsey simply assumed "that the poles with more wires led to a large town." Once or twice she was mistaken, but her commonsense approach got her to California.

48

Uneasy rider. William Howard Taft was the first president to use a car regularly, a White Steamer.

Taft didn't like having his picture taken. When in the steamer, he had a surefire means of avoiding being photographed. As cameramen surrounded the car, his chauffeur, George Robinson, went into action.

Robinson opened a valve that released clouds of steam. While the photographers waited for the mist to clear, Robinson stomped on the gas pedal and the car sped away.

Let's take an old-fashioned walk. The earliest automobiles frightened people and horses alike. Laws that seem goofy to us today were passed to protect man and beast from the dangers of these puffers and chuggers.

The Red Flag Act in nineteenth-century England set the pace. It required self-propelled vehicles to follow not less than sixty yards behind a man waving a red flag during the day and a red lantern at night.

Early in the twentieth century, Tennessee passed a law that put a damper on spur-of-the-moment joyrides. A motorist who planned an outing had to forewarn the public a week in advance by placing a notice in the newspapers.

A 1912 Nebraska law was the wackiest of all. A driver on a country road at night had to shoot off a rocket every 150 yards, wait eight minutes for the road to be cleared, and then drive slowly, tooting his horn while firing Roman candles.

IV

For Hire

Take a tip from me. Part-time cabdriver Benson O'Keefe of Dallas was robbed of twenty dollars by a gunman whom he had driven to a shopping center in 1963.

The gunman gave O'Keefe back a dollar and bragged, "I'm a big tipper."

Bark me a taxi. Moving pets can be a problem. Public transportation won't take them. Neither will most taxicabs.

In Hamburg, Germany, things are different. Animals travel in style. A special fleet of "animal taxis" responds to calls from pet owners.

The taxis are vans equipped with rubber mats, plastic tubs, small cages, and first-aid kits. They transport

dogs, cats, birds, and even horses for no more than the price of an ordinary cab ride. Owners ride free.

Bernd Grundmann founded the service in 1983 with fourteen taxis, the same number that are in service today. The business hasn't made him rich, but it has its rewards.

"The animals are always very quiet," he said. "And not one of our drivers has been bitten."

Kane was able. Nick Kane boarded a cab on his way to work as a carpenter in Miami, Florida, in 1984. Despite a heavy rain, the driver streaked off and whizzed along at 50 m.p.h.

Kane told him to turn. The driver wouldn't even slow down.

Kane shouted at him to stop.

The cabbie's answer was to open the door and jump.

"There I was, going better than thirty-five miles an hour, and nobody was driving," Kane said.

He seized the steering wheel, hopped over the seat, and stopped the runaway cab.

It came out later that the driver had been robbed two months before.

"He thought Kane was another holdup man," a cab company spokesman explained. "He just freaked out."

Classy chassis. The frilliest, fanciest taxicabs ever built hit the streets of New York City in 1910.

Made by the Universal Taxicab Service Company of the Hotel Knickerbocker, the cabs were for nighttime hire only—to carry wealthy passengers to theater or opera or late parties in deluxe luxury.

Each cab resembled a little glass house on wheels. The inside was lit by electricity with reflectors. "Thus a woman," commented *The New York Times*, "on the way to the opera or theatre can not only show off the latest Parisian creation in gowns but her jewels as well."

The cabs were heated, making it possible for passengers to take a wintry ride without wraps. The top was lined with silk. The cushions were of costly damask and brocade.

Larger than the ordinary cab, the supercabs seated six or eight persons. In some of the smaller models, the interior decorations were removable. Hence a woman could order a taxicab in colors to suit her gown.

There's something about a man in uniform. The first motorized force in the history of warfare was a fleet of run-down taxicabs.

Early in World War I, the Germans were closing upon Paris, the French capital. France seemed ready to fall.

French Major General Joseph Simon Gallieni had troops but no means to rush them to the front. He cast about for anything with wheels and came up with a desperate idea.

He ordered the Paris police to flag all the taxis in the city.

The cabbies were told to report immediately to the

Ministry of War, a big, brown, domed building. There army officers sent fleet after fleet of the high, little Renault taxis creaking across Paris to collect waiting battalions.

On September 7, 1914, "Gallieni's taxicabs" rolled out of the city and into legend.

With running boards bent and tires flattened under the weight of the soldiers, the little eight-horsepower Renaults strained over unpaved roads toward the fighting at Marne. As if fueled at the pumps of patriotism, about 660 of them made it.

The fresh troops helped turn the tide of battle and dashed Germany's hopes for a quick victory.

A new career. The taxicab industry was born in 1907 because wealthy, young Harry N. Allen was cheated. The driver of a horse-drawn hansom cab in New York City charged him five dollars for a ride of only three-quarters of a mile.

Allen's companion that February evening was a young lady with whom he had just dined. He did not wish to make a scene. He paid the overpriced fare.

Nevertheless, he fumed over the injustice of it all night. By morning he had made up his mind. He would start a cab service in New York and charge so much per mile.

What's more, he decided to try motorcars. Since American cars did not suit him, he went to France. There he found what he wanted: a small, sturdy car that was cheap to run and that customers would like.

56

He got backers in France and New York to the tune of $3 million. For his share, he coined the word *taxicab*.

"The *cab* part was a natural," he explained. "The *taxi* came from a French company that made meters for horse cabs, called 'taximetres.' That means a meter that arranges for the tax. I merely combined the two."

On October 1, 1907, a fleet of sixty-five gleaming red taxicabs paraded onto the streets of New York City. Many of the drivers were college boys looking for excitement.

The next day *The New York Times* reported the news: "The new taximeter motor cabs, which promise New Yorkers low-priced cab service, made their first trips for the general public yesterday.... Dinner guests of the Plaza Hotel were treated to free rides by Harry N. Allen, president of the new Taxicab company.

"The new cabs are attractive-looking vehicles, 16-horsepower, four-cylinder Darracq cars of the landaulet type made in France. The driver is in uniform not unlike that of the West Point cadet.

"The fare on the taximeter for from one to four persons will be as follows: First mile or fraction thereof, 30 cents; each quarter mile thereafter, 10 cents; each six minutes of waiting, 10 cents."

Harry N. Allen's motorized, metered cabs were a smashing success. Soon he had 700 on the streets. But even as he had soared to fame with his cab company, he fumbled away his place in automotive history. The word that he invented, *taxicab*, delighted him but doomed his memory.

He might today be better known than Chevrolet, Chrysler, Dodge, or Ford—if he had called his metered cab an "Allen."

Nab a cab. Riding in a taxicab in Detroit in the summer can be a sweltering experience. In July 1980, it was hotter than passengers realized.

That month the police seized twenty-three stolen cars that were repainted and put into service as cabs. Among them were eight cars that belonged to the city of Detroit, including three police cars.

Reach out and touch somebody? According to the New Mexico 1985 driver's manual, "It is against the law for taxi drivers to reach out and pull prospective passengers into the cab."

Change for the better. Mrs. Fred Doheny was held in a taxicab in Brooklyn for more than half an hour because she had too much money. Cabdriver Frank Selig refused to change her $20 bill after a $1.50 ride and locked her in.

Selig was fined and put on two years' probation in 1929. The State Court of Appeals ruled that Mrs. Doheny was "effectively imprisoned."

V

There Auto Be a Law

Caradise **lost.** For those who keep track of such mat-
ters, the person from whom the most cars have been
stolen is David Picket of London.

Over a period of eight years, beginning in 1976, he
had fourteen cars stolen. Actually, it was only ten *dif-*
ferent cars; some were stolen twice. No insurance company would write him a policy against theft.

In 1985, the police called Picket and told him they'd
recovered a cassette player lifted from his dashboard.
While he was inside the stationhouse, a thief drove off
with car number fifteen.

Santa's little helper? If your car is ever stolen, hope
it was taken by the same thief who made off with Kelly

Terrell's 1974 Chevrolet pickup truck in December, 1985.

Two months later, Terrell, of De Witt, Michigan, received a telephone call. He was told that his truck had been returned to the parking lot from which it was stolen.

The caller had more to say. He lectured Terrell on the poor condition of the truck and about leaving his keys in the ignition.

Sure enough, the truck was in the parking lot—with the dents removed, a new paint job, and a list of repairs three pages long.

Thanks, but no thanks. In Green Bay, Wisconsin, plainclothes detectives drive unmarked cars with ordinary license plates. Their cover was nearly blown in 1986 when the new plates arrived.

The smart-aleck convicts who made the plates stamped every last one with PD—telltale initials for Police Department.

After one look, Deputy Police Chief Robert Langan shipped back the plates.

"They were," he said, "a dead giveaway."

They just don't make cars the way they used to. The Dumbest Driver Award for 1980 goes to the West Virginia man who tried to rob a bank with his car.

He tied one end of a heavy chain around the handle of the bank's outdoor night-deposit box. The other end

he fastened to his bumper. When he drove forward, the front of the deposit box was supposed to drop off. Instead, his bumper did. On it was his license plate.

The police didn't need another clue to make an arrest.

Plugging the law. Grant Pobihushchi was given a ticket in 1985 for parking too close to a fire hydrant in front of his home in Edmonton, Canada.

Pobihushchi asked the policeman to take a closer look.

The hydrant was painted red, white, and blue instead of the regular Edmonton yellow, and it had chains attaching the caps.

Clearly, the hydrant wasn't a real hydrant. It was a lawn ornament, and it belonged to Pobihushchi.

The policeman looked and agreed it wasn't your average fire hydrant. But the law was the law. He told Pobihushchi to pay the ticket and sped off.

Pobihushchi won the case by staggering into court with some pretty heavy evidence—the 135-kilogram "hydrant."

Escape hitch. A convict named Barry Crosby succeeded in scaling the wall at England's Stanford Hill Prison in 1985. But it wasn't his lucky night.

The car he flagged down for his getaway was driven by an off-duty police officer, Sergeant Peter Holloway.

"As soon as he stepped into the car, I knew he was a prisoner," Holloway said. "I said jokingly, 'I bet you've just jumped over the wall,' and to my amazement, he admitted he had. He didn't know I was a policeman."

The sergeant proved his identity by driving the escapee to the local police station.

The engine died. A stolen 1980 two-door Pontiac went underground at the Crown Hill Cemetery in Tulsa, Oklahoma.

Felix Gonzalez, a worker at the cemetery, was walking his dogs in 1984 when he saw a bumper sticking out of the ground.

Police said the thieves used the cemetery's heavy machinery to dig the hole and bury the car.

The price of swapping. A hitchhiker with a fast fist and a slow brain got a ride from Canadian Burt Mann near Toronto in 1951. By way of saying thanks, he stole Mann's wallet and socked him in the nose for good measure.

Later, he made a discovery. Mann's wallet was empty, and he had left his own wallet, containing seventy dollars, in Mann's car.

He called Mann and offered to exchange wallets. Mann agreed to meet him. The police met him, too, and clapped him in the clink.

Flash, take the bus. While the Atlantic City gambling casinos were beating the suckers out of millions of dollars, the city's police department was going flat broke.

Ten new patrol cars were locked in a city lot in 1985. The police department lacked the money to mount flashing lights on the roofs.

A detective had to take a bus to the scene of a murder because no cars were available.

Next time use the drive-in window. Things went smoothly for two robbers who held up a bank in Shelby, Kentucky, in 1931—until they tried to make their getaway. They ran outside with two sacks of money and found that their stolen pickup truck was gone.

The owner of the truck, R. C. Carney, chanced to be in the area during the robbery. He hopped in and drove away.

The robbers-without-wheels took off on foot. They were caught inside an hour.

What's in a name? Counterfeiters of car titles sealed their own doom in California.

Police had no trouble in spotting the phony titles and rounded up a dozen suspects in 1982.

The counterfeiters (real dum-dums) misspelled the "Great Seal of California." The fake titles read: "Great Seat of California."

Picking his customers. Willie Steinspring, a garage owner in Staten Island, New York, mastered the law of supply and demand in 1929.

Through improper use of an ice pick, he created a demand for his tire-repair services. He was stabbing tires when Patrolman Edward W. Browne arrested him.

Automobile owners in the neighborhood had been complaining for six months about the extraordinary wear and tear on their tires.

VI

Faster, Faster, Faster

Tender is the night. The most thrilling of the early European road races was the Italian Mille Miglia, or 1,000-Mile Race. It was run over roads open to ordinary traffic.

A driver never knew what to expect around the next hairpin turn—an old farm cart, a cow, or a donkey. As dangerous as the mountain roads were by day, they became death lanes in the dark.

Yet in 1930, Tazio Nuvolari stole victory by a trick that bordered on madness. He switched off his headlights!

Night had fallen on the last part of the race, the sprint to the finish in Brescia. Nuvolari, behind the wheel of an Alfa-Romeo, was in second place. He

70

trailed Achille Varazi, who drove a bigger and faster Maserati.

In his desperation to win, Nuvolari flicked off his lights. His car blended in with the darkness. Varazi, glancing back, believed—as Nuvolari wished him to— that his rivals were so far behind him that he couldn't see their headlights. He eased off.

Nuvolari swiftly gained on the unsuspecting Varazi. Two miles from the finish, he turned on his lights, shot into the lead, and won!

How to peddle your car. French automaker Armand Peugeot had a bright idea. To promote his cars, he entered one of them in the 1891 Paris to Brest race— an event for bicycles!

His car completed the race at a speed of about 10 m.p.h. It finished dead last, soundly outclassed by old-fashioned leg power.

Peugeot was heel-clicking happy nonetheless. His car had made the first real long-distance automobile trip. No one had given the newfangled contraption a chance to cover the distance in one piece.

Fast it wasn't, reliable it was. The news boosted sales more than even Peugeot had hoped.

Too close for comfort. The feature race packed Moncrief Park, a racetrack in Jacksonville, Florida, in 1910.

The field was mixed: one man, one horse, one mule, and one automobile.

The man had to race 550 yards; the mule, 990 yards; the horse, 1,320 yards; and the automobile, 1⅛ miles.

Few in the standing-room-only crowd actually favored the latest scream, the automobile. Most rooted for the man, and a few pulled for the mule. In the end, the horse drew the loudest cheers by winning.

The man, Walter Williams, complained bitterly. He, not the mule, should have been awarded second place. Fifty yards from the finish line old long-ears had forced him to dive under the rail to avoid being trampled. His claim was not allowed.

The youngest entry, the automobile, which had brought out the crowd, trailed throughout the race.

Will Overhead won('t). The most unusual "winner" of the Indianapolis 500 never drove in the world-famous auto race.

Fact is, he never lived.

Nonetheless, one newspaper hailed his victory in 1933.

The people of Walsenburg, a coal-mining town in Colorado, chattered with excitement over the story in their daily newspaper, *The World Independent.* It announced that Will Overhead, an unknown, had won the 500.

The rest of America's newspapers printed the truth. Louis Meyer had finished in first place, capturing the second of his three Indy victories.

Who, then, was the mysterious Will Overhead?

Answer: the child of newspaper slang.

In the 1930s, a newspaper could make a special request for a story from the Associated Press, the news-gathering service. The AP commonly sent the story by telegraph.

The slang term for this procedure was *overhead.*

For example, a newspaper might put in a request such as: "Kindly send us story on bishop's arrival tonight." The AP would reply: OK, WILL OVERHEAD BISHOP.

The 1933 Indianapolis race was half completed when the editor of *The World Independent* received his last telephoned report of the day. He telegraphed the AP to rush him a story on the winner as soon as the race was over.

The AP wired back: WILL OVERHEAD 500 WINNER—meaning it would do as requested.

The editor, a newcomer and as green as grass, thought the AP was giving him the name of the winner. The Memorial Day edition reached front porches with the banner headline: OVERHEAD WINS INDIANAPOLIS RACE.

Will Overhead had not been mentioned in the telephoned accounts from the speedway, which covered the first 250 miles. So it was necessary to mention in the story's lead that he came from behind in the last half of the race to win. "The editor was waiting for his big story, the Indy 500, and it was getting close to his deadline," said George Zannon, who set the famous headline in type. "We were going to beat everybody on the story."

They beat everybody. Alas, Will Overhead didn't.

Greatest show on earth. The first official motor-vehicle race in which any contestant finished was held in Chicago in 1895. The winner was Frank Duryea in a Duryea Motor Wagon. He averaged a little better than seven m.p.h. over a fifty-five-mile course.

The automobile was still considered such an oddity that the following year a Duryea Motor Wagon was put on display by the Barnum & Bailey Circus.

It was pictured in the foreground of posters and exhibited as a freak. Crowds flocked to marvel at this carriage driven over the common highways without the aid of horses or other draft animals.

Circus ballyhoo men called it beyond a doubt the most ingenious mechanism ever put into practical use. For once they didn't exaggerate.

Stretchering a point. Disappointment, success, danger, and humor surround racing drivers. For George Robertson, add the word *hospital*.

Robertson had a turn for finishing a race on a stretcher.

Twice he had to be carried off the course of the Vanderbilt Cup, the major event of early American auto racing.

In 1908, Robertson, then 23, finally won the race and the cup. He drove for 4 hours and 48 minutes, covered 258.06 miles, survived a final-lap blowout, and walked away without a scratch. . . .

That night he drove into Manhattan for a celebration dinner with a friend. Getting out of the car, he stepped on a loose manhole cover—and broke his ankle!

Back to the hospital.

Indy first place. The Indianapolis 500 has produced more than its share of oddities. The second Indy, run in 1912, was the oddest of them all. Further, some records set in 1912 still stand, and two of them probably won't ever be broken.

The race seemed a runaway for Ralph DePalma. He charged to the front during the third lap. After 190

miles, he had stretched his lead to more than 11 minutes.

Then, three laps from the finish, his German-made Mercedes threw a piston. His pace slowed from 80 m.p.h. to below 30. The sputtering engine died in the back stretch with less than two laps to go.

DePalma and his Australian mechanic completed the lap by getting out and pushing. The effort was too much. They sagged against the car exhausted, one lap short of the 500 miles.

Nothing in the rules mentioned a time limit for the race. Nothing prevented DePalma and his mechanic from taking a rest before heroically shoving the car around the final lap. There were twelve prizes, and only ten cars remained in the race. But the weary, disappointed driver and mechanic were too spent to push another lap—two and a half miles—for the tenth-place prize of $1,300. They called it a day.

Joe Dawson, driving a National, won the race and $20,000. He set an Indy record that still stands: the winner who led the race for the fewest number of laps —two. DePalma's 196 laps in the lead remain the most for any nonwinner. Because of new rules, his feat of pushing his car can never be challenged.

There was more.

Ralph Mulford, victor in the 1911 Vanderbilt Cup race, clung to last place, miles and miles behind everyone. Nine cars had finished when he drove into the pits. His six-cylinder Knox, plagued by clutch problems, was the only car still running.

As Mulford munched fried chicken, he was told that if he wanted the money for tenth place, he had to complete the 500 miles. He climbed back into the Knox and resumed the grind.

Around and around the winding oval course Mulford nursed the Knox like a man atop four loose wheels. Dawson had won in 6 hours and 21 minutes, averaging 78.72 m.p.h. Mulford took an hour and a half longer as he poked toward everlasting fame. His time of 8 hours

and 53 minutes represents a speed of 56.29 m.p.h., the slowest ever for the Indy 500.

Frenchman's follies. From the beginning, racing drivers vied against one another in a brotherhood of sportsmanship. An exception was the hotheaded Frenchman, Victor Hemery.

In 1906, the best cars on earth assembled on the sands of Ormand Beach, Florida, for an assault upon the world speed records. Hemery was there with a big, powerful Darracq.

There, too, was the sleek *Rocket,* the Stanley steam car driven by Fred Marriott.

Low and streamlined, *Rocket* was a far cry from the boiler and stack mounted on wheels of earlier days. Like any good steamer, it had practically unlimited power and speed.

Hemery looked over *Rocket* with growing concern. It didn't take long to make up his mind. He must get rid of this dangerous rival in the quickest, simplest manner.

As the cars lined up for a heat of the Dewar Cup, the most prized event of the meet, Hemery drove the Darracq close to the steamer. He revved his 200-horsepower V-8 engine. Flames flew from the Darracq's open exhaust stacks, blasting the wood and canvas body of *Rocket.*

The officials threatened to throw Hemery out of the meet. He cursed them in French, a language the Americans didn't understand. Eventually, he was disqualified for refusing to rerun a heat. The Darracq company cabled the wild Frenchman that he was fired.

Fred Marriott and *Rocket* survived the blasts that day and won the Dewar Cup. Three days later, Marriott took the steamer back onto the beach and went after the one-mile record.

Although he approached the starting line rather slowly, he had the steamer hissing between the markers. Man and machine hurtled along the shoreline in a cloud of steam. The result was a world record of 127.66 m.p.h.—18 m.p.h. faster than wheels ever had traveled the distance.

The record was not bettered on sand for twenty-two years, until 1928. After nearly a century, it remains on the books for cars with less than 30 horsepower.

Hemery could only grind his teeth as his rival gathered glory. Worse was to come, for the hotheaded Frenchman's temper had cost him a lasting place in auto-racing history.

His racer, the big Darracq, was turned over to his mechanic, Victor Demogeot. On January 29, 1906, three days after *Rocket*'s fantastic one-mile run, the Darracq outsped the steamer by a split second over two miles.

Victor Demogeot, unheard of a few days before, suddenly held a world record. Averaging 122.3 m.p.h., he had become the first man to go faster than a mile a minute for two miles.

He had won his chance because a countryman had blown his temper and his exhaust stacks.

VII

That's the Ticket

Clothes make the man. Police in Findlay, Ohio, had no suspects in the 1984 kidnapping of a member of the force.

Officer Fred, a mannequin, was taken from a police car. He had been with the department for two years. Dressed in a uniform, the life-size dummy was used to slow down speeding motorists.

"He was a good officer," said Mayor Keith Romick. "I know I slowed down whenever I saw him."

A doozy of a snoozy. A New Jersey traffic policeman was caught sleeping in his patrol car in 1984. He hired a lawyer and an "expert witness," a hypnotist, to defend him.

The policeman, testified the hypnotist, was lulled

into a trance by passing traffic. The trance is called "highway hypnosis," said the lawyer.

The explanation didn't catch the court napping. The verdict: four months' suspension without pay.

Boy, did he get a wrong number. To pay a traffic fine, an 87-year-old man in Columbus, Ohio, mailed the police a check for $2,131.18 in 1983.

After getting the ticket, he had looked on the back to see how much he owed. He thought the amount a little steep, but he didn't fight it.

The number wasn't the amount he owed, but the section of the city code he had violated—2131.18.

Authorities tore up his check, after he paid the proper sum, $25.

Once in a lifetime. Louis Booth of Poughkeepsie, New York, didn't put a coin in a parking meter in 1947. The judge, however, ruled him innocent. The meter had been set up after Booth had parked his car.

Nothing succeeds like succession. In Littleton, Colorado, in 1982, a judge threw out a minor traffic charge against Prince Jelwi Bindullah because the prince was fifty-seventh in line to succeed King Fahd of Saudi Arabia.

Fair is fair. Officer Richard Baker of Hampton, Iowa, accidentally crashed his patrol car into another vehicle

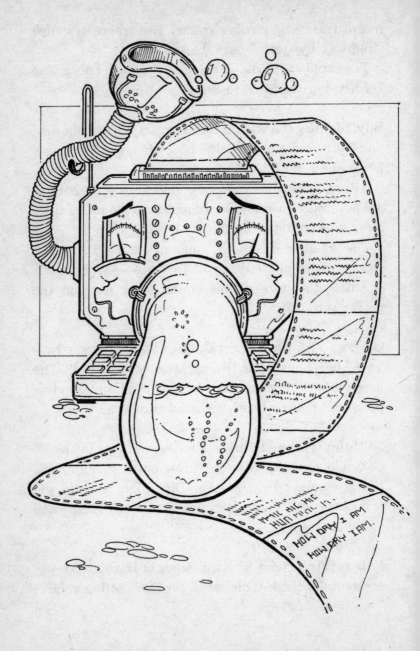

in 1971. For not yielding the right of way, he wrote himself a ticket.

Computers anonymous. Police in Smethwick, England, had to take their new breath-test machine off duty in 1977. It became drunk.

The machine tested drivers suspected of drunkenness by delivering an instant computer readout of blood-alcohol levels. The machine was supposed to replace the old plastic bag, which merely turned green if the alcohol content in the breath was too high.

The minicomputer got tipsy. It began to give readings high enough to indicate that drivers had more alcohol in them than blood. Too heavy a dose of alcoholic fumes had done it in.

"It couldn't take all the alcohol, and we had to remove it," said Chief Inspector Patrick Wallace. "We sent it to the home office to get dried out."

A moving story. In Madison, Wisconsin, two police officers questioned the use of radar to catch speeders.

Anthony Jarona, Jr., and Richard Daley went before the city's police advisory committee in 1980 to air their protests.

The pair had become doubters following tests by a radar unit. A parked car was clocked at 12 m.p.h. and a junkyard at 29 m.p.h.

No one loves a traffic light. In 1867, William P. Eno, 9, was riding with his mother in New York City when

they were caught in a traffic jam. There were only about a dozen horses and carriages involved, but no one knew exactly what to do. It took half an hour to untangle the mess.

Young William never forgot the experience. For the rest of his life he devoted himself to solving traffic problems. When he died in 1945, he was recognized as the leading international authority on the subject.

In 1903, New York City police began using the first traffic control manual, Eno's *Rules of Driving*. Many of his rules are still followed today, such as slow-moving traffic must keep near the right curb; a vehicle that overtakes another must pass on the left; a stop is signaled by raising the hand, and a turn by pointing with the hand.

Eno originated one-way streets, the safety island, rotary traffic, the pedestrian crosswalk, the stop sign, the taxi stand, and traffic cops.

Strangely, the man who is called the "Father of Traffic Safety" didn't think much of traffic lights at first.

"Beware of skillful salesmen trying to sell these devices," he warned city and town officials. "Do not be tricked by them! A mere light will not keep a motorist at an intersection. A traffic officer in his proper station at the center of the intersection will always be needed."

Eventually, Eno realized he was wrong about stoplights, and he came out in favor of them. But throughout his life he preferred horses to motorcars.

The man who was recognized as the leading international authority on traffic control hated to drive. He was driven everywhere by a chauffeur.

Never take anything for granted. Spitting in a limousine owned by Dade County, Florida, carries a $50 fine even though the county doesn't own any limousines.

Don't be half safe. It's against the law in Arizona for a pedestrian suddenly to "leave a curb or other place of safety and walk or run into the path of a vehicle."

Strangers when we met. Gaston, South Carolina, population 1,200, got its first stoplight in 1985. A few hours after it went up, a motorist tried to run the red light and caused a four-car pileup.

Fast talk. Speeders will try just about any excuse to wiggle out of a ticket. The most common is, "I gotta get to the bathroom."

The police have heard most excuses a hundred times, but a few new ones crop up every year. Would you believe . . .

A housewife in California explained that she was running out of gasoline and was trying to build up enough speed to coast to her home five miles away.

A pet-shop owner in Cleveland claimed he was speeding to test a car he was thinking of buying.

A doctor in Massachusetts insisted, "I was trying to get home with a roast-beef sandwich while it was still hot."

A volunteer fireman from Long Island maintained he was speeding to Lenox Hill Hospital just to see how long it would take in case he ever had to drive a patient there.

A hatcheck girl in Hollywood blamed her good looks. "I had to drive fast to keep sailors from trying to get into my car," she said.

After being clocked at 100 m.p.h., a cowboy in San Antonio said he had just left the car wash and was trying to blow-dry his pickup.

A bank clerk in Rapid City, South Dakota, said he was in a hurry to get to a gas station before he ran out of gas.

A driver in Indianapolis said he was going too fast because a bee had flown into the window, and he was preoccupied with killing it. He produced a dead bee as evidence. The police officer inspected the bee and spied dust on the wings. The man admitted that the bee had been dead for months. He carried it around to use as an excuse.

A nurse in Atlanta said she had just received a potent shot at a hospital and the doctors urged her to "get home very fast."

A woman led the California Highway Patrol on a 150-mile chase at 90 m.p.h. and didn't stop till she ran out of gas. She told the officers that her accelerator pedal was stuck.

A truck salesman was stopped for speeding at 90 m.p.h. in a 40 m.p.h. zone near Reno. He claimed he was going into 50 m.p.h. head winds and thought it would balance out.

A teenager in Oakland was pulled over for speeding in a stolen police car. He grinned and said someone had stolen *his* car and he wanted make a citizen's arrest, but he needed something official-looking. So he stole the police car. As with the rest of the excuses, the police officers listened with patient good humor and didn't believe a word.

Only in America. On November 16, 1983, many wore black, but nobody wept as the town of Caldwell, Idaho, buried "Red-eyed Pete."

Pete was the last traffic light to be removed from Interstate 80, the last obstacle to nonstop, coast-to-coast travel.

Three licensed morticians were on hand for the ceremony. Pete, decked out with a pumpkin head and straw arms and legs, was unhung, laid in a horse-drawn hearse, and carried a mile to the grave.

Mayor Al McCluskey delivered the eulogy in poetry. Several hundred people watched the rough wood casket being lowered into the ground.

The gray headstone read: "Here lies Red-eyed Pete, one red light you need no longer beat."

Time on her hands. Lori Lajoie, the only meter maid in Freeport, Maine, quit after a week on the job in 1983.

"Handing out tickets made me feel kind of guilty," she said. "It wasn't bad until everyone started noticing what I was doing. I felt like I was on display or something."

The 20-year-old college student was not replaced. Reserve police officers took over her work of handling illegal parking by summer tourists.

It was an easy switch. "Meter maid" was strictly a Kentucky Colonel type of title. The town had no parking meters.

Writing the wrong. Richard Roderick, a policeman in Plymouth, Massachusetts, was transferred from his downtown beat in 1983 because he wrote too many parking tickets.

Merchants complained that he was scaring away customers.

On one of his better days, Roderick wrote fifty tickets. On another, he ticketed the town's street sweeper.

Park and parcel. New York City is probably the hardest place in the world to find a parking space. No one knows it better than United Parcel Service, and you can say that again. By 1986, the delivery service reportedly owed the city $1.2 million in unpaid tickets.

Time waits for no one. Three members of the federal government went to Allentown, Pennsylvania, in 1986. Their mission: to discuss the city's problem of collecting $9,800 in parking fines run up by servicemen. When they left the meeting, they found a $3 parking ticket on their car.

Cars de ballet. India's only dancing traffic policeman tripped the light fantastic for the last time in December, 1985.

Head Constable Inder Singh Tanwar, 43, gave his final performance at his regular traffic box near Parliament, the busiest, most celebrated intersection in New Delhi. His dazzling display of arm signals and blur of fancy footwork stopped traffic.

When he finished with a heel-click and a bow, he was cheered, mobbed, hugged, and carried around the intersection on the shoulders of admirers.

Over the years, drivers regularly parked their cars to watch him perform. Children showered him with sweets. Prime Minister Indira Gandhi often stopped and applauded.

"I've accomplished my job if I have made people smile," said Tanwar, who ended thirteen high-stepping years without writing a ticket.

VIII

Odd Parts Bin

Standing on the corner. The bus service that tried the hardest to stay on schedule ran between Hanley and Bagnall in England.

In fact, drivers quit stopping for passengers along the route in 1975. Before would-be riders got wise, buses tore past lines of up to thirty people.

"If the buses stopped to pick up passengers, they couldn't keep the timetable," said a bus official.

Are you kidding? Floyd Clymer of Berthoud, Colorado, was America's youngest automobile dealer. In 1906, when he was 11 years old, he started his business in the office of his father, a doctor.

A born go-getter, Floyd billed himself as "the kid agent" for Reo, Maxwell, and Cadillac cars (and for

Thomas, Autobi, and Yale motorcycles). In his first two years he sold twenty-six cars.

As a grown-up, he stayed true to his first love, the motorcar. He founded a publishing company that specialized in books about automobiles, motorcycles, and motor racing.

Space shot. Finding a parking spot in San Francisco isn't easy. It took Harry Guyton nineteen years.

In 1966, Guyton worked for the prosecutor's office. He put his name on a waiting list for a space in a downtown, city-owned garage. He guessed that he might have to wait a few months.

One day his telephone rang. The voice at the other end said that a parking space was his.

The news arrived a mite late—in 1985. Guyton had been retired for two months.

It loses a lot in the translation. Donald Carroll, an American tourist, rented a car in Tokyo, Japan, in 1984. In the glove compartment he found a booklet of instructions. It was written in Japanese-English . . . or possibly English-Japanese. A sample paragraph:

"When a passenger of foot heave in sight, tootle the horn. Trumpet at him melodiously first, but if he still obstacles your passage, then tootle him with vigor."

One in a million. A Central State College exchange student from Iran was looking for a car in 1960. He walked into a showroom in Edmund, Oklahoma.

Scarcely able to speak English, he was ripe to be cheated by a shady dealer. But the owners of the dealership, Craig Ayers and Bob Ford, gave him a fair deal.

The student, Bob Azarmi, remembered.

Fifteen years later he was the buyer for the Iranian Contractors Association. He placed an order with Ayers and Ford for 750 dump trucks and 350 pickups.

Weather wise. John Gosson of Syracuse, New York, decided it was too cold for him to drive around on his motorcycle during the winter.

In 1983, Gosson, a car mechanic, stuffed $7,500 into his leather jacket and zoomed off to buy a new car.

On the way the cash flew out of his pocket. He recovered only $3,240.

A month later Gosson received a postcard from San Francisco. It read: "John, weather's great. It took me a while to find out who to thank for this great vacation . . . it was like seventh heaven picking and gathering loose bills on the highway. Having a great time. Sincerely, Thankful."

Grumbled Gosson, "The guy's gotta be a jerk."

They only come out at night. They talk ugly trucks in Austin, where since 1984, the Ugliest Pickup Truck in Texas contest has been held annually at the Hog Eye Bait Shop. John Kelso, an Austin newspaper columnist, dreamed up the event. He keeps the rules simple. There are no entry forms or fees. A truck has only to come and go under its own power to qualify.

102

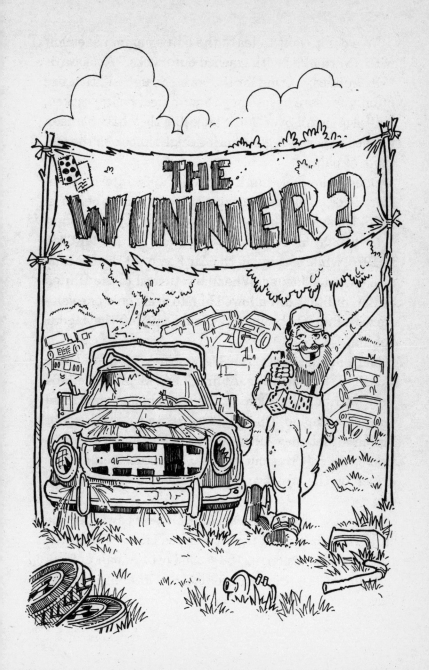

"We don't want to leave the bait-shop management with a yard filled with trashed-out trucks," Kelso says.

Pickups competing for the coveted "ugliest" title are fit only for sore eyes. They're wrinkled, bent, cracked, and sagging all over. Most look like they haven't been washed in years. A good hosing might knock off the last spots of paint.

Doug Celovsky's hunk of junk, a 1966 International Harvester, won over seventy-one other mess-heaps in 1985. He said his life had been changed by the honor.

He bought his truck at a scrap yard in Italy for $350 in 1976, while serving in the Air Force. At the time, he also owned a Jaguar. When he returned to the United States, military law allowed him to bring only one vehicle with him. He brought the truck and left the Jaguar behind.

His entrance into the Ugly Truck Hall of Fame wasn't all easy cruising. At first, Leon McMahan's 1964 Ford with a bullet hole in the windshield was named Grand Champion. The judges were so busy checking for ugliness that they failed to notice McMahan's inspection sticker. It was out of date. The truck couldn't be driven on the street and so was ineligible for the contest.

Celovsky, who had finished second, was awarded the title. He didn't mind that it was too late to switch the top prizes. He preferred the second prize, a pair of foam dice, to the first prize, eats for two at a local taco palace. Classy.

Like tires, like feet. Can women's feet go flat from riding in autos?

Dr. H. L. Goldwag feared so. He was no small bunions, either. As chairman of the scientific committee of the New York State Pedic Society in 1930, Goldwag warned the nation to beware of "automobile foot." Too much riding, he asserted, was causing women's tootsies to weaken and spread like root beer on the Minnesota Flats.

Eyeball benders. How a driver sees a space depends on his or her body shape, according to a British researcher.

Short, chubby men and women are likely to underestimate their width—and their cars'—and will try to squeeze through spaces that are too narrow, says Arthur Crisp. Result: rumpled fenders.

On the other hand, tall, thin drivers tend to overestimate their width and that of their cars and will usually hesitate or stop in front of a gap in traffic. Result: *pow!* from the rear.

The back of my neck to you. School bus drivers in California got tired of making empty threats like, "How many times do I have to tell you to *sit down?*" So in 1984, they went to school to learn assertiveness.

The popularity of the three-hour course came as no surprise to Karen Finkel, executive director of the National School Transportation Association. She considered driving a school bus a high-stress occupation.

"Show me a teacher who would spend an hour with his or her back turned on a room full of ninety kids," she said.

Beats a banana split. Doreen Nowlan of Uxbridge, Massachusetts, bought a car for 999 bananas.

Nowlan was listening to radio station WMRC in 1984, when she heard a King Ford-Mercury ad. The pitchman, "Crazy Carlo"—in real life, Carl Bengiovanni, the dealership's general manager—announced

that he'd sell a car for 999 bananas.

Nowlan, 24, thought it was a joke. After fifteen minutes, curiosity got the better of her. She had to find out. She called the owner of the Milford dealership, James Peltekis.

Peltekis was shaken. Everyone knows "bananas" is slang for dollars. But an offer was an offer. He stood by it.

Nowlan peeled off 999 bananas and got the car, a 1975 green Peugeot that Peltekis said was worth about $2,000. The Salvation Army got the bananas, worth about $120. King Ford-Mercury got publicity throughout the United States and Europe, worth about a million dollars.

It was a fruitful deal all around.

The sensational Scandina diet. Felice Scandina of Sicily walked into a hospital in 1952. He complained of a bellyache.

After a brief examination, he was hurried into the operating room. Doctors removed twenty-eight penknives from his stomach, plus half a dozen metal coins, eight metal keys, three silver spoons, and bits of glass.

Scandina, 21, said he had been "training" to make good a boast that he could eat an automobile—windows, doors, tires, and all.

Ballet Russe de Monte Car-Go. You can see a boardwalk in lots of places. But if you wanted to see a car dance, you had to go to California.

A group calling itself the Gulf Farallones put on the dances, beginning in 1983. Members first combed San Francisco for a parking lot—er, rather, a stage—that had a "really potent emotional mood." They finally chose a bus lot beneath a huge coffee sign.

On a busy night, theatergoers drove up, and those with reservations got a place on the edge of the lot. The only lights came from performing cars waiting on the sidelines to go on.

Cars rolled onto the stage singly or in groups. They circled, interwove, flashed their lights, shot out of the lot, sped around the block, and returned. They raced directly for the audience in a clanking chorus line and stopped with a squeal of brakes. They "danced" with live actors or by themselves.

"They work together in an amazing way," declared Karl Danskin, 27, the leader of the dance group, following a 1985 ballet by an old Dodge pickup and four Japanese imports.

One of his scriptwriters, Melinda Mills, wrote a piece about a woman who lived with her baby in a 1971 Chrysler Newport. Like most of the car dances, it was deeper than it appeared. Mills explained the meaning to puzzled viewers.

"My goal is to balance the spiritual aspects of people with cars," she said.

In 1983, the car dances won an award from the Bay Area Theater Critics Circle honoring "new directions in the theater."

110

Despite the recognition, the group didn't grow rich. The actors had to dance their own cars. They received only $10 a performance, plus gas money. The top tickets sold for $4, less than a tenth of the price of a Broadway show.

The 1985 season was the most successful financially. A private fund donated $1,000. With that and $4,000 from ticket receipts, the group just about broke even.

If I tolled you once, I tolled you a thousand times. Toll collectors on the Maurice J. Tobin Memorial Bridge in Boston collect money and hard-to-believe stories.

One collector, Paul Thomas, a twenty-six-year veteran by 1984, gave as good as he received. When a driver asked, "How do I get to Harvard?" Thomas had a standard answer.

"Study," he told them, "study."

Champ for a day. In 1984, John Tee attended a U.S. Customs auction of seized and abandoned goods in Norfolk, Virginia.

"Sometimes you get a good deal," he said with a broad grin.

For $15, Tee bought a 1972 Mercedes Benz 280S, a late-1970s Volvo 264 GL sedan, and a Guzzi motorcycle —a $9,600 value.

You think you've got it bad? Thomas Hammond crawled into an old Pontiac in the Chicago Police Department Auto Pound in 1978 and fell asleep.

The noise of metal being crushed awakened him. By the time he realized *what* was being crushed—the old Pontiac with him inside—it was too late to escape.

He screamed, but his screams were drowned out by the surrounding snap, crackle, and pop.

Presently, the Pontiac and nine other squashed cars were loaded onto a flatbed truck. Hammond continued to scream for help, but by now he was too hoarse to make himself heard.

The truck headed for a wrecking yard in nearby Summit. Along the way, a passerby noticed a hand sticking out of one of the cars. The police were alerted.

At the wrecking yard, police and firemen rescued Hammond from the crushed Pontiac. It was the next in line to be shredded.

Hammond was sped to Community Memorial Hospital in La Grange. A spokeman said he didn't appear to be seriously injured, and added, "He could use some sleep, however."

Get a horse! According to New York City's Department of Transportation, the average speed of a horse and buggy in midtown Manhattan in 1907 was 11.5 m.p.h.

Today, too many jaywalkers, too many cars, and too many angry cabbies clog the streets. The average speed of a motor vehicle is 9.8 m.p.h.

The horses still average 11.5.

Progress—it's wonderful.

Solution

Monroe Burnside was the guilty boy. He, not Conway Tintushel, had stolen the ashtray.

Monroe said he saw Conway "sneaking out the back door" of one of the police cars.

Impossible!

He did not know—but Encyclopedia did—that police cars do not have inside door handles on the back doors. They are removed so that prisoners can't escape.

Trapped by his own words, Monroe confessed.

No one but Conway bid on the ashtray. He took it home for fifty cents.